Spaced out

Spaced out

A comprehensive guide
to award winning spaces in the UK

Nicola Garmory and Rachel Tennant

AMSTERDAM • BOSTON • HEIDELBERG • LONDON • NEW YORK • OXFORD
PARIS • SAN DIEGO • SAN FRANCISCO • SINGAPORE • SYDNEY • TOKYO

ELSEVIER

Architectural Press is an imprint of Elsevier

Architectural
Press

Architectural Press
An imprint of Elsevier
Linacre House, Jordan Hill, Oxford OX2 8DP
30 Corporate Drive, Burlington, MA 01803

First published 2005

British Library Cataloguing in Publication Data
A catalogue record for this book is available from the British Library

Library of Congress Cataloguing in Publication Data
A catalogue record for this book is available from the Library of Congress

ISBN 0 7506 6142 9

For information on all Elsevier publications
visit our website at www.elsevier.com

Typeset by Charon Tec Pvt. Ltd, Chennai, India
www.charontec.com
Printed and bound in Italy

Contents

Acknowledgements

Many thanks to everyone who helped and inspired us on our journey.

Particular thanks to Patrick Goode for his advice and editing skills and to Zuzana Sebinova for her patience and help.

Photographs by Rachel Tennant.

About the authors

Rachel Tennant is a landscape architect and keen photographer and has travelled throughout the world photographing natural and built landscapes.

Nicola Garmory and Rachel Tennant are co-directors of the successful practice TGP Landscape Architects. They have both travelled extensively around Europe studying and researching designed landscape spaces.

They are also co-authors of *Professional Practice for Landscape Architects* published by Architectural Press.

Introduction

Public spaces are designed. They don't just happen: they are formed through a considered process of planning, survey, analysis, design and implementation.

This book will give you an insight into some such spaces in the UK.

Chosen from a number of projects throughout Britain which were recognized for their special qualities, the 31 spaces in this book were selected from a shortlist of awards over the past 10 years. These are the combined work of design professionals including architects, planners, landscape architects, urban designers, artists and engineers.

There are many awarding authorities throughout Britain now, but we chose the following National Awards as being the most relevant to the designed environment:

The Landscape Institute Awards
The Civic Trust Awards
The Royal Town Planning Institute Awards

These awards are described on the following pages.

For each space, we have aimed to give you an idea of its type and character, where it is or how to get there, a brief description and why it won the award, with some comments from ourselves on our thoughts and feelings about the design. An abridged version has been provided with regard to the judges' reasons for making the award.

Our tour of Britain was interesting and rewarding but we soon realized that not all well designed spaces won awards. The award winning spaces depended very much on a client or designer initially submitting the place for an award. There are a vast number of projects throughout the UK where good design has not been recognized through a formal, national award and have therefore not been included in this book.

There again, there were award winning spaces which we visited but chose not to include in this book due to the fact that they looked unmaintained, or were suffering from damage or vandalism or we considered them not to be up to a standard that we would aspire to.

In just 31 examples chosen, one can experience huge variations in the design, use of materials and context of the spaces. It was refreshing to see the use of water in so many places, something that adds focus and fun to a space. Also the use of soft materials in city centres and urban squares brought a brightness and interest to the urban environment, particularly the use of grass and herbaceous material. Spaces do not exist on their own, the success of a space depends on the context, the surrounding buildings or environment and the people using it. It requires to exist as an entity in its own right as well as fitting in with the surroundings, it requires an energy and a concept that is easily translatable by those using it.

The National Awards

The Landscape Institute Awards

The Landscape Institute promotes the highest standards in the practice of landscape architecture and management.

The Landscape Institute Awards are held to honour excellence and innovation in landscape architecture and presented to encourage and recognize outstanding examples of work by the landscape profession. The awards aim to bring greater awareness of the best contributions from Landscape Institute members in creating an improved environment. Our main focus has been on the design category.

The Royal Town Planning Institute Awards

The Royal Town Planning Institute was formed to advance the science and art of town planning for the benefit of the public.

The RTPI established its annual awards for Planning Achievements in 1977. The purpose was to throw a public spotlight on the achievements of the town planning profession. The awards recognize the diversity of planning achievement, whether in urban or rural areas, large or small scale, involving new developments or regeneration and promoted by the public, private or community sectors.

The Civic Trust Awards Bi-annual Awards

The Civic Trust promotes progressive improvements in the quality of urban life for communities throughout the UK. It is Britain's leading charity, devoted to life in Britain's cities, towns and villages. The places where people live, work, shop and relax.

The Civic Trust Awards scheme is the largest and most comprehensive environmental design awards scheme in Europe. It has been established for 45 years, during which time it has become highly respected for recognizing architectural and environmental design that makes an exceptional contribution to our environment. The Civic Trust Awards are unique in that they do not simply award good design, but also take into account the way in which schemes relate to their settings and to the people that they serve.

Location of Spaces

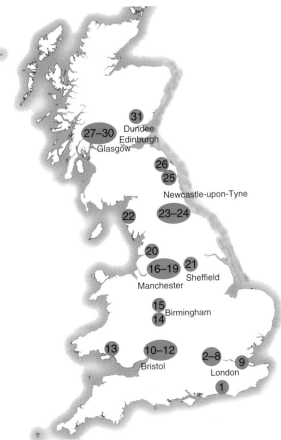

1 Brighton Seafront PHASES 1–5
2 Trafalgar Square
3 Royal Victoria Square
4 Greenwich Peninsular
5 Thames Barrier Park
6 Cutty Sark Gardens
7 Triton Square
8 Russell Square Gardens
9 Ingress Park, Greenhithe
10 Bristol Harbourside and Legible City
11 At Bristol
12 Queen Square
13 Millennium Wetland, Llanelli
14 Phoenix Square
15 Victoria Square
16 Cathedral Gardens

17 Exchange Square
18 Castlefield
19 Salford Quays
20 Warrington Town Centre
21 Heart of the City
22 Whitehaven
23 Grainger Town
24 International Centre for Life
25 Amble Regeneration
26 Alnwick Market Place
27 Dynamic Earth
28 The Hidden Gardens
29 Cathedral Precinct
30 Homes for the Future
31 Dundee City Centre

Brighton Seafront

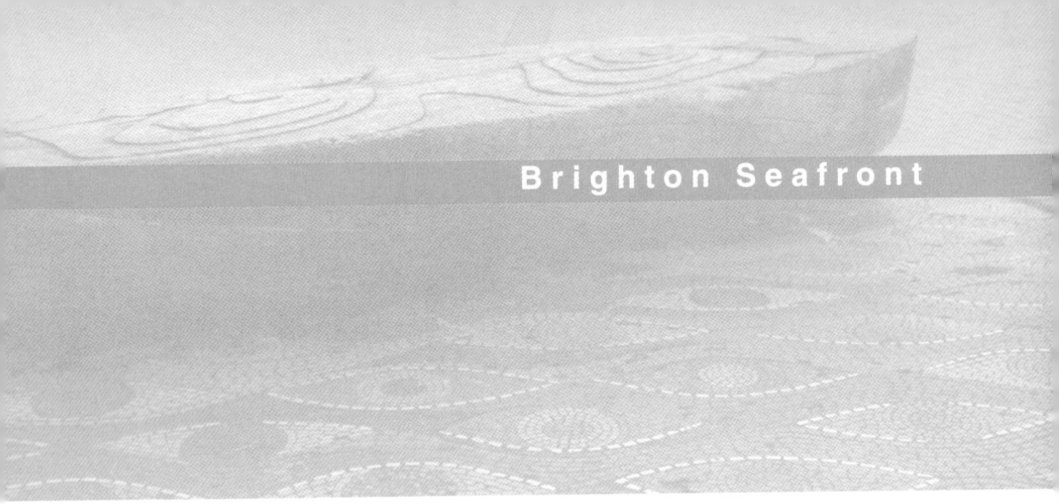

1

Brighton Seafront PHASES 1–5

Space Type
A Seaside Town Waterfront
Location
Seafront, from the Brighton Pier to the Hove boundary
Award
Civic Trust 2001

Description

Until 2001 this stretch of seafront was run down. Extensive environmental improvements have resulted in a waterfront which now plays an important part in the life of Brighton. The lower promenade has widened, new shops, cafés and artists' workshops have transformed the old 'arches', and artworks have been introduced. The design theme is a 'string of pearls' along the seafront taking on board the historic theme, focusing on the fish market and fishing museum, leading on to the artists' area, nightclubs and bars, while Hove has more of a family bias. A strong curvilinear form is expressed in the path and boardwalk, linking the 'pearls'. A series of features and artworks such as volleyball and basketball courts, performance spaces, etc. are integrated into the design. In the recently completed Phase 6, children's play is the major theme.

Judges' views

"This is an ambitious and impressive landscaping scheme that has been extremely successful. The design is bold and full of character and surprise, yet subtle in its detailing and use of materials. All in all, it seems totally appropriate for the city that is unique in its flamboyance and cultural richness".

Designers

Brighton and Hove Council Conservation and Regeneration Team.

Comment

Although not part of this award, we have included Phase 6 as it formed an important and integral part of the space as a whole. Even on a dull day the area is full of vibrancy, bustling with people. It is an effective design of a linear space with a good use of simple basic materials and unusual original detailing of some features. The whole process has extended the town to the beach and now includes sailing, food and drink sources, sport, fishing, shopping and play, both during the day and night.

2

Trafalgar Square, London

Space Type
An Urban Square
Location
City of Westminster, Central London.
Nearest tube: Charing Cross
Award
Civic Trust 2004

Description

The 2004 improvement project has improved pedestrian access and enjoyment of the area whilst enhancing the settings of its buildings, monuments and spaces. Traffic has been redirected away from the north side of the square, connecting the National Gallery and providing the building with a plinth. The square has been enlarged and redesigned with traditional materials. Recycled nineteenth-century granite that was originally part of the north terrace retaining wall has been used for walls and balustrades. Access for disabled and servicing has been boldly incorporated into the design using glass boxes with frames of brown bronze.

A modern touch has been introduced with the use of contemporary designed benches using details of bronze from the same foundry that supplied metal for the two lion sculptures built in the 1860s at the foot of Nelson's Column.

Judges' views

"Overall it is an extraordinary contribution to the environment, creating an urban space that is representative of its true potential and role in the capital".

Designers

Foster and Partners, Atkins Design Environment and Engineering.

Comment

A hugely popular space, thronging with people all year round. The new design achieved a successful, robust and large-scale improved space reflecting the status of this world-famous square. The good thing about the improvements is that they fit in well and could, in fact, always have been there. The link with the National Gallery has opened up the square and created better pedestrian movement. The large slabs reflect those used throughout the rest of the space whilst the new seating, café areas and lifts introduce a modern element which brings the space into the twenty-first century.

Royal Victoria Square

3

Royal Victoria Square, London

Space Type
A Modern Urban Square

Location
The Royal Docks, adjacent to the Excel Centre, London.
Nearest Station: DLR Custom House

Award
Landscape Institute 2004

Description

On the northern edge of Victoria Dock, this 1.6 ha site, conceived by London Docklands Development Corporation, was designed to provide a hub for leisure, business and residential developments and to connect with existing communities. The design evolved from the site's existing features such as the buildings, cranes and waterfront setting. A central lawn is bordered by a paved walkway. The canopy is punched through with names of ships that docked in the old basin. Materials reflect those used in past industrial times – steel, natural stone, concrete and timber. The fountains provide a ceremonial route to the Excel Centre and a play facility for children.

Judges' views

"This understated scheme sets an inspirational benchmark for contemporary urban landscape design. The project has real presence, scale and attention to detail and geometry and represents the best integrated landscape design. The scheme is deceptively simple but compels users to engage with its routes, views and experiences. The combined effect of paving, structures, lighting and planting creates a memorable landscape that is forward looking, well-built and a highlight of the gritty dockland setting".

Designers

EDAW, Aspen Burrow Crocker, Patel Taylor.

Comment

This site may have been 7 years old when we saw it, but it appeared not to have achieved the use and status that was probably anticipated. Unfortunately when we viewed the space, the 'dancing fountains' were not working and there were no people to enliven it. This may be more to do with the context of the square as a forerunner to future surrounding development than the actual design. We also found that the space leaks out, it is not bound by built or natural elements and therefore the eye is drawn to the expanse of water and undeveloped spaces beyond.

4 Greenwich Peninsular, London

Space Type
A Series of Parks Connected by a Riverside Walkway
Location
Adjacent to the Millennium Dome, North Greenwich, London.
Bus from Greenwich or tube from North Greenwich
Award
Civic Trust 2002

Description

The central, southern and ecological parks were established as part of an initial masterplan for the whole peninsular after the closure of the gas works and the proposal to use the site for the Millennium Dome. The central park has been designed on the basis of a 7-metre grid, establishing numbers of trees and widths of paths, and forming a rhythmic and modernist landscape. The boundary to the paths with its granite linear seating and block planting of lavender and lilies, ivy and avenue of trees creates a simple and effective design solution. Beyond the row of industrial cottages and Pilot Inn is Southern Park with its memorial to the employees of the Southern Metropolitan Gas Company who died in the two world wars. At the other extreme, the ecological park adjacent to the colourful Greenwich Village is designed with lakes, boardwalks and wetlands. A haven for wildlife with woven willow screens and bird hides which both protect the birds and allows viewing of them too. All three parks have high-quality street furniture and lighting and offer full access for people with disabilities.

Judges' views

"The innovative and sensitive treatment of these areas has set a standard for future developments of the peninsula".

Designers

Desvigne and Dalnoky: Central Park, WA Atkins;
Nicholas Pearson Associates: Ecology Park, Bernard Ede.

Comment

A bold and striking development complementary to the size and scale of the Millennium Dome. The formality of the two central and southern parks contrasts well with the informality of the Ecological Park. Modern design elements such as the granite seating are strong features which channel movement through the main areas of the parks. The monoculture of herbaceous planting, lavender for instance, is very effective in the summer when flowering, but may look less appealing throughout the winter months.

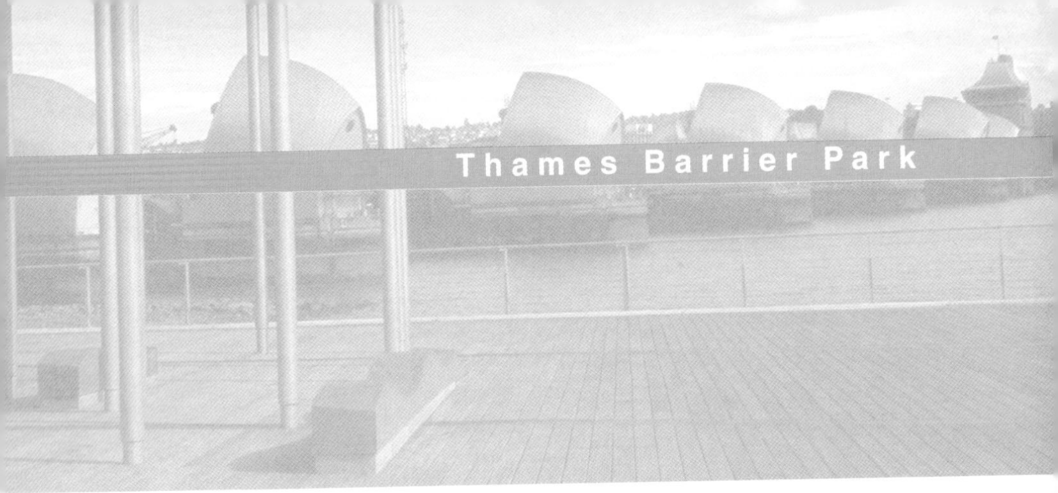
Thames Barrier Park

5 Thames Barrier Park, London

Space Type
An Urban Park

Location
North Bank of The Thames, North Woolwich Road, Silverton.
London Docklands

Award
Civic Trust 2002

Description

A former industrial site lying north of the Thames Flood Barrier. This nine hectare park, developed following an international design competition, is both urban and contemporary with references to the past history of the site. The Sunken Green Dock (reference to the former Prince Regent Dock) is a remarkably designed long and narrow channel cutting through the park at an angle, containing a rippling wave of yew, and lines of herbaceous and shrub planting follow the line of the cut.

At the river side there is a vast timber deck with wave-shaped seating and a pergola dedicated to those killed in the two world wars.

To the north of the sunken gardens is an area surrounded by huge concrete walls banded with black slate and filled with a geometric pattern of 36 water jets.

Bridges of steel tubing and graphite iron railings cross the cut.

Elsewhere the park offers contrasting uses with a large lawn, a wildflower meadow, a riverside walk and a traditional playground.

Judges' views

"Already this new park seems to be having a very positive impact on the surrounding area, which is rapidly being developed into housing. During the last half-century the value of green space – both social and commercial – has been forgotten and few new parks have been created. It is hoped that this innovative and beautifully designed park will act as an exemplar and that in future the creation of public parks will be included in regeneration strategies as a matter of course".

Designers

Groupes Signes, Patel Taylor, Arup

Comment

A clear and bold landscape concept which is still fairly unique to British park design. It is a beautifully designed, implemented and maintained park. Attention has been given to the wider design and to minute detail. The views and vista created within the park are spectacular. The park is used well despite the fact that it is very difficult to find and the entrance is currently hidden from public view. The opening up of the new docklands railway station will surely make this park a very popular all year round destination.

6 Cutty Sark Gardens, London

Space Type
An Urban Riverside Square
Location
Greenwich
Award
Civic Trust 2000

Description

The Cutty Sark is a major tourist attraction and World Heritage site. The area around the ship has been improved and transformed to create a square worthy of its status. The space is a setting for the ship itself, a viewing platform for the River Thames and a point of transition (as the ferry terminal and Brunel's rotunda are built within it). The square consists of an area of elevated decking with a red painted entrance wall and signage, interpretation boards built into the distinctive timber boundary fencing and an area with banners and columns. Generally the materials are man-made but there are traditional stone setts around the Cutty Sark which reflect the historical status of the ship.

Judges' views

"This important riverside space has been transformed by a simple yet highly effective hard landscaping scheme using wood decking, yorkstone paving and well-engineered handrails and street furniture. The severity of the design forms an admirable setting for the strong lines of the Cutty Sark and nearby Gypsy Moth, while ensuring that this busy riverside area is an appropriate gateway for visitors to this historic town".

Designers

Timpson Manley Ltd., Dewhurst McFarlane and Partners.

Comment

The red painted wall and timber interpretation boards are a strong introduction to the square with bold use of colour and materials. The timber decking and steps create a maritime feel and a good means of dealing with level changes. However, the materials specified have not stood up to the use and abuse by so many visitors in this very popular tourist location and the space is looking tired and worn in places.

Triton Square

7

Triton Square, London

Space Type
A Contemporary Urban Square
Location
Regents Place, off Euston Road.
Nearest Tube: Warren Street.
Award
Civic Trust 2004

Description

A new urban space, which acts as a centrepiece within a new mixed use development. The design is based on an extension of the building grid onto the landscape and also the theories of geomorphology. The design of the seating and surrounding retaining wall with *wavy* turf boundaries reflect this. Portland stone and granite are predominant surface materials. The lighting columns are strong features along the main Euston Road but the surface lighting is also very effective.

Judges' views

"The square integrates well with its surrounding landscape, taking elements and reference from it. Light is used as a central landscape design element and, as a result, the space is particularly effective in the evening and has developed into a popular 24-hour attraction and destination. The lighting, layout and design has had an extremely positive impact on its environment, adding great vibrancy to the area, and perceived as a sculptural experience in its own right".

Designers

Sheppard Robson, Ove Arup and Partners, Edco Design Ltd.

Comment

A contemporary space with a pleasant atmosphere and well used for both sitting and passing through. The simple design includes strong elements such as the spiral seating and the lighting columns along Euston Road. The site is banded by curved crisp granite walls, lime tree avenues and plains of short mown grass and ivy.

The ornate ancient frieze and raised feature trees on top of the columns appear fussy and conflict with the rest of the designed space.

8 Russell Square Gardens, London

Space Type
An Historic Landscape Garden
Location
Off Southampton Row, Bloomsbury.
Nearest Tube: Russell Square
Award
Civic Trust 2004

Description

The existing Humphrey Repton designed Grade 2 registered historic landscape garden has been conserved and enhanced. Sensitive arboricultural work to the mature London planes, restoration of the statue of Sir Francis Russell, restored boundary railings and the introduction of a modern fountain in place of the original 'garden hut' have contributed to the overall upgrading and enhancements.

Judges' views

"Using archive material, original survey plans and archaeological trial pits the missing elements of the original design were restored. Renovation of the café was also incorporated into the project ensuring that the new building became part of the landscape through using materials that were natural and sympathetic".

Designers

Land Use Consultants.

Comment

The gardens have been restored in a sensitive manner, retaining the historic character of the design and including new elements from the original plan such as herbaceous gardens and an avenue walk. The implementation is low key and subtle. The café and fountains are a huge focus and attraction to the space. The interpretation boards at key entrances are an added bonus to the garden experience.

9   Ingress Park, Greenhithe Waterfront

Space Type
Waterfront and Historic Parkland

Location
One mile east of the Dartford Bridge in Greenhithe

Award
RTPI 2001

Description

Once a large area of derelict ground and an historic estate of Ingress Abbey, now a new mixed development. The 29-hectare site started as a major clean-up programme, many features and materials were recycled and the Capability Brown parkland restored. The framework plan focused on the site's urban design opportunities and created eight distinct character areas reflecting the existing identities. The resulting landscape includes the creation of a waterfront path and associated spaces, waterside park, countryside linkages and areas of public realm of distinct character and quality augmented by the good choice of materials.

Judges' views

"The challenge was to produce a development which respected the historic landscape, incorporated the listed structures and responded to connections with existing communities. We were impressed by the first phase of the housing in the Village Heights which demonstrates the way in which a high quality public realm is strongly defined at the entry point and along the frontages. A tight palette of materials has been used which relates to the local vernacular in a way which provides an urban feeling and a development of real character".

Designers

Tibbalds TM2 and MW Landscape

Comment

The design contains good detailing and use of materials with quirky features and artworks within the public realm. There is a good use of recycled materials combined with new materials. The planning process and designer's 'eye' is obvious through the conservation and creation of views and vistas from the Abbey and the impressive views along the waterfront.

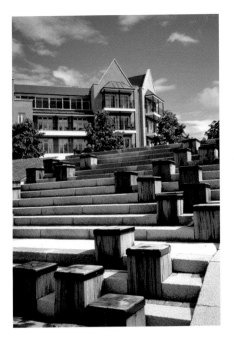

10

Bristol Harbourside Regeneration Project and Bristol Legible City

Space Type
A Series of Waterfront Spaces and Linking Streets and Paths
Location
Bristol City and Harbourside
Award
RTPI Planning Award 2001

Description

A development framework for **Bristol Harbourside** was prepared jointly by Bristol City Council and urban designers 'Concept Planning Group' and a new revitalized series of spaces were created which included:

- Newly designed Queen Square
- At Bristol
- Anchor Square
- The Centre Promenade
- Pedestrian bridges
- Connecting paths, streets and water front spaces.

The total harbourside now has a sense of vitality and is an essential part of Bristol's day and night life with cafés and bars lining the waterways. Artworks are prolific and enhance the street life and water life of the area.

The Legible City initiative is an integrated programme of arts projects and transport information to improve people's understanding and experience of the city and is obvious in the harbourside redevelopment.

Judges' views

The judges were "pleased to see all ages enjoying the fountains and water features of the public spaces and were impressed with the high standards of materials and quality of the environment. It has produced a standard that other public areas will need to aspire to".

"We are particularly impressed by the use of specially developed maps using three-dimensional building images that people can easily recognize. The project is about creating an easily enjoyable well-connected environment. It uses a visual language of easily understood symbols and legible text which enhances people's understanding and enjoyment of the city by raising their environmental awareness".

Designers

Bristol City Council.

Comment

A mixture of traditional and modern design features all forming a bustling active waterfront both during the day and at night. The use of water in the squares is innovative and exciting. The variety of designs by different designers and architects adds to the flavour of this new part of the town.

The new signage is distinctive, easy to understand and aesthetically pleasing.

11 At Bristol

Space Type
One Large and Two Smaller City Squares
Location
Cannons Way, off Anchor Road, Bristol Harbourside
Award
Civic Trust Award 2002

Description

The award was won for the two new buildings, 'Wildscreen' and 'Explore', and the surrounding spaces of Millennium Square, Anchor Place and Anchor Square at Canons Marsh in Bristol.

Millennium Square is a bright, contemporary, well-designed and implemented public space with seating, planting and art works including a series of shallow water terraces by the artist William Pye, and light work by David Ward and Martin Richman. Natural elements are predominant and include French limestone, structures are clad in terracotta with zinc roofs and the seating is a sustainable hardwood. Standing and seated figures provide some of the sculptural elements.

The square is integrated into pedestrian routes to the other new spaces, Anchor Square and Anchor Place.

Judges' views

"As a whole the project has contributed to the development of the city".

"Throughout, high quality materials and sensitive contemporary design have created an urban complex of varied form that has revitalized this part of the city".

Designers

Alec French Partnership, Acanthus Ferguson Mann, Michael Hopkins and Partners, Wilkinson Eyre Architects, Balston and Co. and Roger Griffiths and Sons.

Comment

The square is beautifully designed and implemented with good use of materials and lighting. The spaces complement the modern design and scale of the surrounding buildings. All features are very well used and the unusual water features are a huge attraction for play.

12

Queen Square, Bristol

Space Type
A Historic Town Square
Location
Off Princes St and The Grove, The Old City, Bristol
Award
RTPI 2003

Description

Originally one of England's largest Georgian squares until a dual carriageway was driven across it in 1936. In 1993 the road was closed, and in 1998 the authentic and detailed recreation of the square began, using the original designs and layouts. Buses have been rerouted, broken pavements made good, streets resurfaced with cobbles, boundary walls and fences restored. The original gravel path layout and Grade 1 listed statue of 'William the Third', at the square's centre, have all been brought back to their original splendour.

Judges' views

"The physical changes are impressive. The authenticity of the detailing has resulted in a high quality environment. The removal of the buses from the access road and of forecourt parking has enabled the character of the square to be reinstated. The restored square is a triumph for positive planning over inertia and we believe it merits an award for the built heritage."

The Designers

Bristol City Council Planning Department.

Comment

This space has an atmosphere of serenity and simplicity and is well used by many types of people picnicking or resting on the lawns or just walking through. The design is simple yet bold. The retention of the mature trees has held the classic framework of the square. The floor space does not compete with the surrounding architecture of elegant Georgian style buildings.

13 Millennium Wetland, Llanelli

Space Type
A Seaside Waterfront
Location
Coastal Park, Llwynhendry, Llanelli
Award
Landscape Institute 2001

Description

This 76 hectare site is a key part of the larger Coastal Park. The Wetland was reclaimed from poor-quality farmland lying behind the sea wall originally and now combines habitat creation with public access, including a wide promenade, landscape interpretation and art features. All aspects of the project have a multiple, sustainable use, for instance water from the adjacent sewerage works is cleaned and recycled, earthworks are sculpted to contain lakes and to protect wildlife, the mounds also direct circulation and views. There are elements of art throughout which act as such things as viewing platforms, shelters, etc. all using sustainable and recycled materials.

Judges' views

"This sensitive intervention forms part of the ambitious Millennium Coastal Park which is helping to transform miles of derelict industrial land that formerly separated Llanelli from the sea. The Millennium Wetland is a key component of the wider strategy and has evolved into a considerable visitor attraction. The palette of materials is restrained and appropriate. The work of artists is incorporated with subtlety and the scheme suggests quality announcing a particular and special place. The designers have recognized where the detailing needs to be crafted carefully and where it does not. It is encouraging to find an absence of excessive fussiness. Overall, the project recognizes the landscape in which it is located and works within this to achieve excellence".

Designers

Chris Blandford Associates.

Comment

The area is simply designed with solid, robust materials of stone, timber and steel which suit the use and the setting of the space.

The viewing areas, seating and shelter are cleverly placed and implemented to provide sufficient features without becoming overly fussy.

The sculptures along the promenade reflect the same robust functionality but provide due aesthetic relief and interest along the waterfront.

Millennium Wetland, Llanelli 55

The Phoenix Centre

14   The Phoenix Centre, Coventry

Space Type
A Series of Town Spaces and Connecting Walkways
Location
Off Coventry Ringway (A4053) Swanwell, Fairfax St, Hales St and
Trinity St Area, Coventry Town Centre
Award
RTPI 2003

Description

Phoenix has transformed an area of low quality, randomly distributed post-war commercial developments in the town centre into a revitalized townscape.

This exciting new development includes the following new features:

- The dramatic twin arch structure and a glass bridge at the entrance to the town
- Public artworks with the theme of friendship and international friendship in the main Millennium Square
- Restored Lady Herbert Gardens
- A contemporary square with café and water feature surrounded by new apartments at Priory Place
- A historic cloister with pleached lime trees and seats and in particular a vocal art theme of 'Voices from Coventry'
- A space-age overhead walkway linking all spaces through 'the walk of 1000 years'.

Judges' views

"We were impressed by the considerable skill and ingenuity that has gone into planning and developing the project, which connects and regenerates important parts of the city centre. We admire the way the project has been reworked and the vigour with which it has been pursued. Even at the construction stage it was possible for us to get a feel for the quality of the new public spaces and the likely impact of the pedestrian route".

Designers

Masterplanner/Architect: MacCormac Jamieson Prichard; Landscape Architects: Robert Rumney Associates

Comment

The whole area is an intelligent mix of history, innovation and imagination. Each element or space within the project has its own distinct character but all are pulled together by a common theme and high-quality design. The Millennium Square was the only space we found disappointing; a sea of greyness too dependent on the strong lighting pattern. The contrast of the colourful hi-tech walkway and bridge structures between the historic gardens and squares is impressive, as are the incidental art features and sculptural intervention.

15 Victoria Square, Birmingham

Space Type
A Traditional City Square
Location
Off New Street, Birmingham City Centre
Award
Landscape Institute 1995

Description

Victoria Square is an active thoroughfare and a place for sitting and relaxing. Well used by locals and tourists alike, the space has a sense of tradition with a high-quality design and is enhanced by the backdrop of the surrounding historic buildings. The main feature is the sandstone stepped fountain with rippling water and giant 'Dhruva Mistry' bronze river goddess sculpture.

Judges' views

"This is a significant new civic space in the heart of Birmingham which is both a meeting place and a point of orientation. The form and mood of this space contrast with the busy linear surrounding streets which are dominated by traffic. The sight and sound of the water are calming and attractive, as is the impressive scale of public art which forms a major feature of this public space".

Designers

The Landscape Practice Group, Leisure and Community Services, Birmingham City Council.

Comment

The square is now 10 years old and well-preserved; it is extremely popular, and built with traditional, high-quality stone and brick materials which are strong, lasting and robust. The changes in level are integrated well by the planters, steps, terraces and cascades of the water feature. It is a space that enhances the surrounding historic buildings with a grand scale of artwork that fits well. Seating is accommodated by means of purpose-built seating, steps and terrace walls and on a hot summer's day, in this popular square, there is no vacant space. Trees around the two sides form a soft boundary to an otherwise hard city space.

SURFACE GLITTERED OUT OF HEART OF

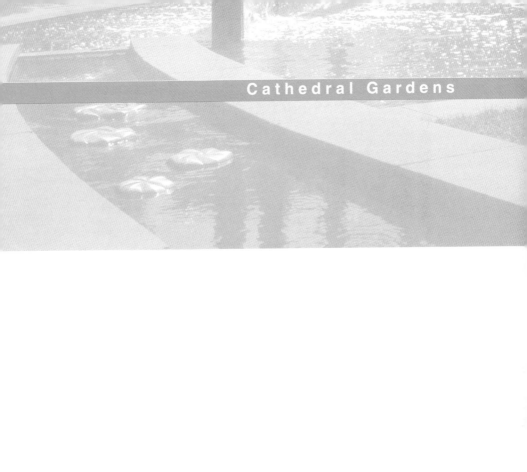

Cathedral Gardens

16

Millennium Quarter, Manchester.
Cathedral Gardens

Space Type
A City Centre Park

Location
Adjacent to the Urbis Building between Todd Street and
Long Millgate, City of Manchester

Award
Civic Trust 2004

The Millennium Quarter in Manchester encompasses four
projects (two buildings and two spaces). The regeneration
of the area was given extra impetus following the bomb
damage of June 1996 and was completed in time for the
Commonwealth Games in 2002.

Description
The Urbis Building stands in the Cathedral Gardens, a city
park used by workers, shoppers, visitors and school children.
The gardens reflect the significance of the historic location.
Following the slope of the ground, the gardens are mainly
grass surfaced with tree planting and features making use of
the sculptural formation of the ground. A water feature along
one edge culminates in a fountain.

Judges' views
"The challenge of the brief has been fulfilled while also
providing a place for quiet contemplation. The landscape is
effectively simple and develops the themes of lawns and
planting within a modern idiom. The design successfully
resolves various level changes and creates inviting public
platforms for multi-functional use. A range of artworks and
water features are integrated into the scheme and the overall
result is a quality, contemporary public garden".

Designers
Building Design Partnership

Comment
The water feature, which is a simple rill with distinct
sculptural elements within it, makes excellent use of the site's
sloping aspect and ends dramatically with the fountains.
There are some bridge features which act as seating and
sculpture within the garden. Whilst the concept is strong
and the use of a lawn is a great relief in the harsh city
environment, the space is suffering due to over use. The
sculptural details and artworks bring an extra dimension to
the space.

17 Millennium Quarter, Manchester. Exchange Square

Space Type
A City Square
Location
Exchange St, Corporation St, Manchester City Centre
Award
Civic Trust 2004

Description

Exchange Square is a triangular-shaped public space created by the closure of a through road creating a triangle in between the Old Corn Exchange and the new Marks & Spencer building. The line of the historic 'Hanging Ditch' is reflected in a water feature lined with stepping stones. The space is designed to provide informal seating for public events through use of parallel ramps defined by walls to utilize the changing levels.

The windmill sculptures were designed by artist John Hyatt.

Judges' views

"Those involved have created a contemporary city space which reflects the past and looks forward: something that people like and use, and has reawakened public pride". The judges felt it should be commended for its vitality, aspiration and optimism and as a testament to the vision of the city council.

Designers

Martha Schwartz Inc, MEDC, Ian Simpson Architects, Hurd Rolland Partnership, Building Design Partnership and Urban Solutions.

Comment

A great example of new and innovative design in the city centre. This original concept brought the use of water back into cities. The steps and terraces are designed to accommodate the changes in levels. The introduction of some major artworks has had a great impact on the space. However, the square is very popular but suffering badly from poor maintenance and repair work.

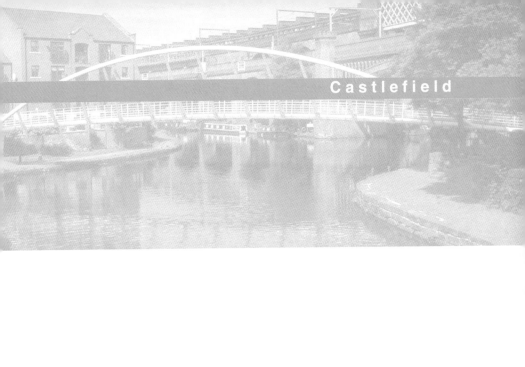
Castlefield

18 Castlefield, Manchester

Space Type
A Series of Waterfronts, Parks and Streets
Location
Northwest of Deansgate, Manchester
Award
Civic Trust 2002 Special Award

Description

Castlefield is a unique mixture of Manchester's history, containing Roman remains, canals and railways. Since 1979 when the area was designated a conservation area, work has taken place to open up canals and create pedestrian connections, restore individual buildings, provide environmental improvements and street lighting, and create public attractions and new developments within the existing fabric of the area. It has now been designated as an Urban Heritage Park and is a successful quarter of Manchester City.

Judges' views

"The success of Castlefield is a testament to the substantial achievements of the organizations involved. Through hard work and long-term commitment, Castlefield has become one of the great success stories in the regeneration of Manchester".

Designers

Manchester Development Corporation.

Comment

The whole area has become totally connectable with ease of access for pedestrians and vehicles and is a joy to move through. Traditional designs mix with new squares and improved spaces. New bars and restaurants have opened up along with many loft type developments. Sculpture and interpretation have added to the tourist interest in the area, describing the industry and the history. The improvements have also encouraged locals to inhabit and use the area safely during the night and day.

Salford Quays

19 Salford Quays, Manchester

Space Type
A Series of Waterside Developments
Location
Salford Docks, off Chester Road, Manchester
Award
RTPI 2000, Civic Trust 2002

Description

The Salford Quays Development Plan was published in 1985. The aim was to create a unique new city quarter, all of it in some way related to the water and the docks of the Manchester Ship Canal. Some components were to be vast and open and others closed and secluded. Water basins have been cleared, new roads and services provided and private investment, with offices and houses, hotels, a cinema and pubs, have been built creating a space for inner city working and living. The best known symbol of the Salford Quays is the Lowry Centre (a cultural centre to integrate the visual and performing arts) and the associated Millennium Plaza which has been designed for outdoor performance using natural paving and robust furniture.

Judges' views

"The transformation of the derelict former Manchester Docks to the Quays of today reflects a civic and professional achievement of a high order. It is the standard and imaginative content of that plan that has been perhaps the most important factor in securing successful regeneration which was later to be reinforced following a review plan by the addition of Metrolink and the centre for performing art 'The Lowry'. Salford Quays reflects civic and professional achievement of the highest order".

Designers

Shepheard, Epstein and Hunter, Ove Arup and Partners.

Comment

Whilst there is a huge variety in development types and designs throughout, the overall space is large, open, bright and generally interesting. The presence of water in and around the whole area, whether part of the canal or in man-made lagoons, lifts what could otherwise be dull and mundane. The Lowry Centre and the War Museum are two buildings of note and are connected by a well-designed footbridge over the Manchester Ship Canal. The Millennium Plaza reflects the scale of the Lowry Building and augments the architecture to provide a space using simple man-made materials.

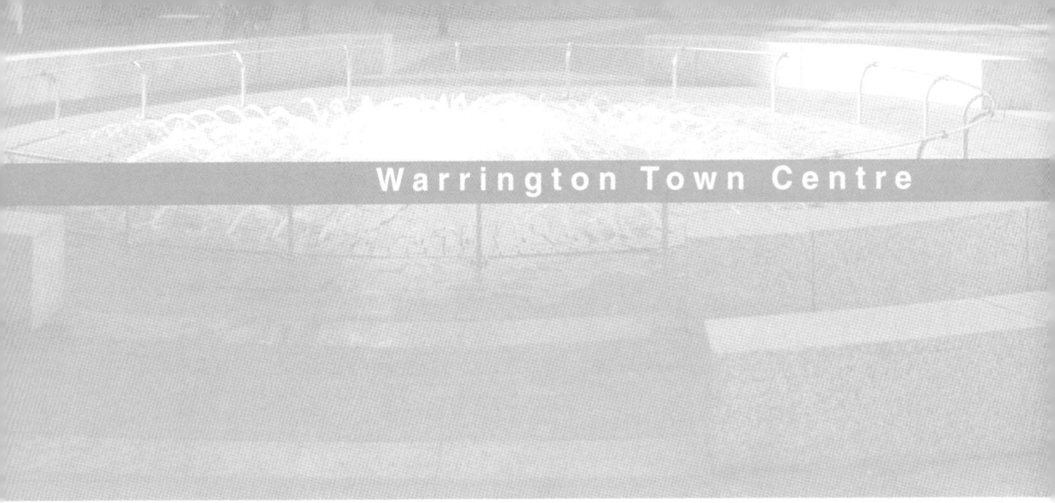
Warrington Town Centre

20 Warrington Town Centre

Space Type
Town Centre Streets
Location
Marketgate, Horsemarket and Buttermarket, Warrington
Award
RTPI 2002

Description

A national design competition was won by Landscape Design Associates along with the American artist Howard Ben. The concept was to reduce traffic and to create a focus and gathering space linked by a series of 'commons' or garden spaces intended to make a pedestrian thoroughfare by transforming the street into a meandering walkway. Marketgate is the physical and civic heart of Warrington. At its centre is a 'well of light' and the 'circle of guardians' which is a water feature surrounded by ten 4 metre patinated bronze columns topped with glass and lit at night. Radiating out from this point is the Horsemarket with a series of themed gardens formed with granite walls and steps, vegetation, trees and columns at the entrance. The adjacent Buttermarket comprises themed commons formed with trees, walls and steps.

Judges' Views

"We were impressed with the quality of the scheme and its originality. The result is an example of strong planning framework and urban design for the public realm at its best that merits this award. Art has been used in a creative and attractive manner to provide focus and the use of original materials and planting, together with a high maintenance regime, should ensure the effect is long-lasting and sustained".

Designers

Landscape Design Associates.

Comment

This streetscape has been designed with a huge amount of attention to detail and the result has been implemented immaculately. The design has a strong traditional theme throughout but with a contemporary feel to it. It could be considered to be 'superimposed' and not to fit into the character of the town, giving it a slightly surreal feeling. The use of 'gardens' of herbaceous plants and shrubs provides a refreshing design approach to the streets.

21 Heart of the City, Sheffield

Space Type
City Square

Location
Adjacent to the Town Hall and within Hallam Square, Sheffield

Award
Civic Trust 2000

Description

The Heart of the City project encompasses the Peace Gardens, the Town Hall entrance and New Hallam Square.

The Peace Gardens have been designed to provide an impressive and popular public square aiding direct pedestrian movement and circulation. The scheme includes a comprehensive lighting scheme to allow night-time use, displays of herbaceous plants, water features and a new fountain.

Judges' views

"As a whole, it succeeds because of the quality of design and materials, and a commitment by the City Council to maintain it. Peace Gardens Square, in particular, provides a catalyst to encourage people back into the city centre".

Designers

Sheffield Design and Property.

Comment

This whole space is exciting, memorable and people-friendly. The day we visited the space it was a honeypot for bathers and picnickers! Designed using stone sett and slab paving, copper gateway sculptures, copper and granite benches and unique flower theme cascades and rills incorporating leaves, pods and stems in green ceramics. The water design is a fantastic contribution to a city space.

Shrub and herbaceous borders are beautifully designed. Raised lawns are well-used and well-implemented.

Whitehaven

22 Whitehaven

Space type
A Seaside Town Waterfront

Location
Whitehaven Harbour, off New Road

Award
RTPI 2001

Description

Once an historic settlement in a run-down mining area, now a revitalized visitor destination.

An improved link between town and harbour, traffic improvements, new housing and restoration of the Georgian heritage and an overhaul of the harbour image are the main elements of the Whitehaven Development Company's strategy. This has been achieved through a lock controlled harbour creating a marina and commercial fishing harbour. Also a series of environmental improvements along the seafront, the most striking of which is a new wave structure along 'Lime Tongue' culminating in a crow's nest. Other improvements include a series of pedestrianized areas using traditional materials and a strategy of public art with a maritime and historic theme, including steel fish on the pavement surface, fish-shaped cycle stands and whale-shaped seating.

Judges' views

"A creative and positive planning approach has encouraged and supported the generation programme and ensured that good quality works have been undertaken. The renaissance of Whitehaven is an outstanding example of how a small community with a population of only 26,000 and in a peripheral location can be transformed by determination and attention to quality though a multi-sector partnership".

Designers

Building Design Partnership.

Comment

The fun, original, and sometimes humorous artwork, makes this space so special. The whole area has a traditional but quirky feel with a maritime theme and historic interpretation. A strong concept, but with sensitive use of materials whether old or new. The improvements really add to the character of the town. The wave feature is a focus and identity within the harbour and creates a destination for visitors, whilst the whole space throngs with people on a hot summer's day.

23 The Grainger Town Project, Newcastle

Space Type
Urban Streetscape

Location
Grey St, Grainger St and surrounding streets in Grainger Town, Newcastle

Award
RTPI 2003

Description

The overall challenge for this area of Newcastle in 1997 was to transform a congested district with poor environmental qualities and vacant premises into an attractive locale for business, residents and visitors. EDAW's study initialized the birth of the Grainger Town Partnership, which led to a series of physical changes to the city streets through pedestrianization improvements including stone paving, customized street furniture of stone, metal and glass, security cameras, artworks and lighting.

Judges' views

"We congratulate Newcastle City Council and its partners for their achievement in regenerating Grainger Town, saving and restoring its architectural heritage and creating such a wonderful example of urban renaissance. The scale of the task was immense. The project provides a model for cities and towns in this country and overseas in demonstrating how a partnership approach, a clear vision involving all sectors of the community and economic, social and environmental and physical programmes, can successfully change and transform a city quarter".

Designers

Southern Green, Insite, Gillespies

Comment

Silver grey granite and Caithness stone slabs pave the streets of Grainger Town. The attention to detail is good. There is a well-designed set of street furniture, using stainless steel, stone and glass. Seats are stainless steel and stone with etched glass uprights including artworks with the theme 'nine things to do on a bench' which adds individuality and humour to the streets. As with many inner city spaces, the design has to be strong and vandal-resistant and, whilst the stone paving is solid and the general street furniture is robust, there was evidence of damage to the litter bins which look quite vulnerable.

meet as rivers
and dance down
towards the
larger sea

24

International Centre for Life and Times Square, Newcastle

Space Type
City Square
Location
Neville Street, Newcastle
Award
Civic Trust 2002

Description

The concept of the International Centre for Life emerged out of the Newcastle University's pre-eminence in the field of genetic research. Times Square was the first new public square in Newcastle for over a century. Planned around a robust and flexible collage of buildings, the focus of the attention at the heart of the scheme is the square. Black and white granite blocks form bold stripes across the top of the square and adjacent to the main building is a more intricate pattern of stone 'crazy paving' and a trail of red surfacing.

Judges' views

"The construction of this centre of excellence for genetic research has aided the regeneration of this area. Architecturally, the building acts as a response to its surroundings – the curved forms of the layout reminiscent of the sweeping forms of the railway lines. This is truly a civic project".

Designers

Terry Farrell and Partners, Mott McDonald, Gillespies.

Comment

From a distance the black and white stripes of the surfacing contrast well with the yellow coloured walls and modern concrete seats around the square. At close quarters the quality of implementation and maintenance of the surfacing and features within the space is poor. The DNA sculpture is a strong and meaningful feature and the old sandstone building of the 'Cattle Market Office' retained in the centre of this space is a strong contrast in age and scale to the massive, contemporary and curvaceous building of the Life Centre itself. It is a shame that the quality of implementation does not do justice to the design concept.

Amble Regeneration

25 Amble Regeneration, Northumberland

Space Type
Town Square and Streetscape Improvements
Location
Amble Town Centre
Award
RTPI 2002

Description

The scheme includes a community resource centre, a new town square, street improvements and reconstruction of derelict areas. The new town square with its memorial garden is not only designed to attract children and visitors but makes a vital link between the town and the waterfront where remodelling of the promenade, restoration of an old jetty and construction of a tidal barrier have taken place. The square itself is the main focus alongside improvements with a central sundial, amphitheatre and interpretative trail.

Judges' views

"Amble is an outstanding example of regeneration of a small seaside town through the involvement of a wide range of agencies. It is a clear demonstration of partnership working to achieve a vision of the future in which the whole town has been fully involved. We could see that the original strategy enabled a vision to be set, the development trust to provide delivery of important initial projects and the partnership to maintain the momentum".

Designers

Jane Derbyshire and David Kendall Ltd.

Comment

In the Town Square materials are fussy and cluttered. The Amble sundial and historic trail, with concepts by local children, are its saving grace and have been meaningfully designed with interesting results. The space is well looked after and maintained but, despite the fact that it was the height of summer when we visited, not very well used.

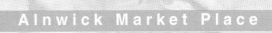

26 Alnwick Market Place, Northumberland

Space Type
Town Square
Location
Off Market Street
Award
Civic Trust 2001

Description

The-800-year old square, in the past used for bear and bull baiting, was until recently a sea of tarmac used as a car park. The use of recycled stone setts and yorkstone paving have changed the nature of the space completely. The improvements include the reintroduction of the historic 'Freemans Path', a diagonal path across the Market Square. This area is now used for events such as the weekly farmers' markets, and the Alnwick Fair and Music Festival.

Judges' views

"Given to the regeneration scheme that has most strengthened the town's role as a service centre while respecting and enhancing its character. This beautifully designed and thoughtful improvement scheme was the result of a successful partnership between many local organizations".

Designers

Reavell and Cahill

Comment

A bustling market square and market cross refurbished in a traditional manner. Materials are natural, stone setts and paving complement the historic nature of the space and its modern-day use. Each seat in the square has been designed with a different theme which provides a sense of ownership and individuality. The interpretation board on the sites history of the space is also a useful feature. The square works well in its own right and is an attractive and well-designed space. The introduction of the market and its associated activities really brings it to life.

27 Dynamic Earth, Edinburgh

Space Type
Modern Amphitheatre

Location
East side of Edinburgh adjacent to Holyrood Palace and the
Scottish Parliament

Award
Civic Trust 2000

Description

The external space complements the unusual structure of
the building on this sensitive site adjacent to the imposing
rocky landscape of Salsburgh Crags. The stone terraces and
steps, closely mown lawns and the clipped yew hedges of
the amphitheatre are the main elements of the design.

Judges' views

"It would have been easy to produce an anonymous structure
or one that was inappropriate or overbearing. The designers
have avoided both with an unusual design that sits beautifully
within its context, an eye catching yet harmonious addition to
both urban and rural landscapes around it".

Designers

Landscape Architects: The Paul Hogarth Company.
Architect: Michael Hopkins and Partners.
Engineers: Ove Arup and Partners.

Comment

A bold landscape design which balances with the strong form
and scale of the building and the impressive landscape
beyond. The main entrance is crisply designed, well executed
and functional. The amphitheatre is a place to sit and view
the bustling city and newly constructed Scottish Parliament
buildings.

28 The Hidden Gardens, Glasgow

Space Type
Public Garden

Location
The Tramway, Albert Drive, South Side of Glasgow

Award
Civic Trust 2004

Description

The Hidden Gardens were designed with close involvement of the local community and local artists. It was converted from a wasteland on the south side of the City of Glasgow adjacent to the Tramway Theatre to create a garden of high quality innovative design to reflect the different cultures of the area. The park has been split into a series of spaces of different characters and includes seating areas, native planting and a shelter, a semicircular pond and secluded lawn, herbaceous borders and integral artworks.

Judges' comments

"A peaceful, high-quality urban landscape and pleasant environment has been accomplished in a deprived area of the city, providing a focal point for the neighbourhood. The interaction with the community forged at the early stages of design has been successfully continued with a wide range of public activities taking place throughout the year and local volunteers involved in the upkeep of the garden. The honest and simple connection between the materials used and the various areas of the garden results in an understated and ultimately extremely successful urban space".

Designers

Landscape Architects: City Design Co-operative. Artists include Divya Bhatia, Julie Brook, Alex Hamilton Finlay, Gerry Loose and Steven Skrynka.

Comment

A magical haven in the city used by locals and visitors, each area has developed its own function and is used in a variety of ways, whether for contemplation or activity. Innovative use of good quality materials, superb perennial planting design and use of native species provides a special place both educationally and aesthetically.

29 Cathedral Precinct, Glasgow

Space Type
A Historic Town Square
Location
The High Street, East End of Glasgow
Award
RTPI 1996, Civic Trust 1991

Description

Originally split by a road and parking area, the cathedral precinct has been formed to make sense of the space between the cathedral, the neighbouring Royal Infirmary and the recently built Museum of Religion.

A new town square has been formed, creating a beautiful setting for the cathedral and a focus for tourists and visitors to the city.

The space has been designed to fit in with the materials and history of the area, using a strong and meaningful paving pattern with granite setts and yorkstone slabs, bordered by lines of trees and seats to define the space while incorporating existing statues and features.

The artist Jack Sloan produced the unique lighting columns using Glasgow's theme of the bell, the fish and the tree.

Judges' views

"This is a sensitive transformation of an important area of townscape. With exceptional attention to detail, craftsmanship and choice of materials, the scheme faultlessly achieves everything it has set out to do.
A tremendous sense of place has been created through the discreet use of good quality materials and a careful attention to geometry. In all respects, this scheme is an exemplar of modern civic design".

Designers

Ian White Associates, Page and Park, Crouch Hogg Waterman.

Comment

This space has a sense of timelessness reflecting the atmosphere of the cathedral and the Necropolis beyond. Despite being adjacent to a busy road junction, Cathedral Precinct has a peaceful feel about it. The design is an exercise in simplicity but with overwhelming impact. It is a highly visited place by crowds of enthusiastic tourists, but there is always a corner where quiet contemplation of the surrounding grand architecture can be achieved.

Despite the well-meaning intentions of the local authority, the tiered black planters with fussy perennial displays, placed down the centre of the space, do not augment the design but detract from its simplicity.

30 Homes for the Future, Glasgow

Space Type
Public Gardens
Location
Greendyke St, Adjacent to Glasgow Green,
The East End of Glasgow
Award
Civic Trust Award 2002

Description

This project was the core part of a programme of events celebrating Glasgow as the UK City of Architecture in 1999. It was conceived as a way of using derelict areas to reconnect the city centre to the East End. The gardens have been designed to allow private and public access around the site and to augment the innovative design of the buildings. Design includes granite sett paving, mainly native tree and shrub planting, a distinctive steel and wire pergola and modern concrete seating.

Judges' views

"This is a showcase of innovative architecture designed by seven different architects. A flexible set of design guidelines ensured that the historic nature of the site was respected while encouraging creativity and innovation. The new urban environment maintains its identity through a design connection between blocks, yet also provides an exciting variety of techniques and aesthetics".

Designers

Turnbull Jeffrey Partnership, Elder and Cannon, Rick Mather Architects, Ushida Findlay Architects, RMJM, Wren Rutherford, Ian Ritchie Architects.

Comment

This is a well kept secret garden just off the busy High Street and Glasgow Green Park. The lush tree and shrub planting and the introduction of contemporary elements, such as a pergola and modern seating, unite the external space with the built form, but also soften and contrast with the hard planes of the architecture.

31

Dundee City Centre

Space Type
A Streetscape and Pedestrianization
Location
The Town Centre including High Street and Overgate
Award
RTPI 2000

Description

Dundee City Centre has been transformed from a traffic congested, pedestrian-unfriendly area with poor shopping frontages to a traffic free space. It has been repaved with high quality materials such as Caithness stone, granite and whin, together with public art designed to reflect the local history and culture expressed in street furniture, various surfaces and street sculpture.

Judges' views

"The new Overgate makes an outstanding contribution to the regeneration of the city centre, attention has been given to shop fronts and housing, as well as to pedestrianized areas and transport, and there are many examples of excellent detailing in street furniture and pend gates. All this has visibly enhanced the city centre experience and supported economic resurgence. The judges are in no doubt that Dundee City Centre Improvements fully merit an Award".

Designers

Gillespies.

Comment

The town centre improvements have provided an exciting new environment for the users of the town. Street patterns and colours of materials have reflected the surrounding buildings, whilst street furniture and artworks have introduced an element of Dundee's history into the street scene, such as the humourous Desperate Dan sculpture, gateway banners and 'twists' from the city's textile past.